To Judith

Lowly Manger—
Empty Tomb

greetings o Blessing

[signature]

Lowly Manger—
Empty Tomb

E. ALAN
ROBERTS

Pentland Press, Inc.
England • USA • Scotland

PUBLISHED BY PENTLAND PRESS, INC.
5122 Bur Oak Circle, Raleigh, North Carolina 27612
United States of America
919-782-0281

ISBN 1-57197-152-1
Library of Congress Catalog Card Number 98-068273

Printed in the United States of America

To Doris—Thank you for all the encouragement and inspiration that has enabled me to persevere. You have instilled confidence in me and stimulated the release of my creative ideas.

I would like to acknowledge the background of appreciative comments expressed by colleagues in our Church. They have used my poems in various aspects of Christian worship. This has helped to crystallize the concept that my writing can be used in ministry.

Contents

Foreword

"A poet's word is worth a thousand pictures," according to Elie Wiesel, a poet, playwright, novelist and Nobel prize winner. Waggish people, of course, are quick to add, "Just make sure it's a *poet's* word." In *Lowly Manger—Empty Tomb*, we have a poet's word. Alan Roberts exhibits throughout his collection both the artist's touch and the saint's heart.

Concerning the latter, I am eager to declare it has been my privilege to have Alan as a colleague for years. He has consistently displayed a heart possessed by the Spirit of Christ and a mind that thinks in conformity to the gospel. Discerning and compassionate, perceptive and persistent, gentle and courageous, Alan has loomed among Christ's people as someone who has moved ahead of most and now beckons them to "come to the knowledge of the Son of God, to maturity, to the measure of the full stature of Christ." (Eph. 4:13)

And now to head and heart, to love of the gospel and love for Christ's people, Alan has added hand as his pen has forged new expressions of gospel-experience as surely as a diamond etches glass. Sensitively entering into the bewilderment of Mary, the embarrassment of Joseph, and even the "wagging ears" ("my tongue did what my tail used to do") of a dog, Alan has revisited the Christmas and Easter stories from the standpoint of several different narrators.

Needless to say, however, in his retelling the "old, old story" he has rendered it fresh. C. S. Lewis once remarked that people don't need to hear something new nearly as often as they need to be reacquainted with something old. While Lewis' point is unarguable, it must always be remembered that the reacquainting must strike the hearer as other than old, lest messenger and message be dismissed together.

Take and read this book. You will find yourself startled, then moved to ponder new dimensions of "the faith which was once for all delivered to the saints." (Jude 3)

Rev. Dr. Victor A. Shepherd
Streetsville United Church

1

Prophecy Of Light

They promised a Messiah
    to enlighten the darkness.
They foretold an event
    that would shatter the gloom.
A Savior will be given
    to safeguard God's chosen.
A Redeemer will come
    to gather His elect.

Such a hope,
    'midst a time of depression.
A noble prophecy
    while God's people were held captive.
      We long for peace,
      we desire release.
          But dare we listen?
          Or dare we hope?

The Prophet is clear,
    no doubt he's sincere.
He listens to God
    and speaks for our good.
The Messiah will come
    in the form of a babe.
A virgin's conception
    is required for God's child.

When He is born,
    He'll be known as God's Son.
        He'll be Emmanuel,
        God living with us.
He'll be the Deliverer
    long sought and awaited.
He'll be the Light
    and scatter all darkness.

They'll call His name
    Jesus—
    the Savior.
        He'll be the Light
        of our present world.

Mary's Response

I am your servant, Lord!
What else now can I say?

To me you spoke—
       the promise to me you gave.
The promise the Prophets spoke about,
      of the One
      who would redeem us,
      save us,
          purge us of our enemies.

Is he the One of whom you spoke
      to me through Gabriel
      your angelic messenger?
The one who spoke so clearly
      of your promise
      and your choice?

He told me not to fear.
He said,
      "God holds you dear,
         you are lowly;
         He'll be holy.
Yes, Mary,
You are highly favored."

Deeply perturbed;
      I wondered—
         perhaps
         I should be more wary.

He spoke again—
Again I shook.

    "Your son—

    God's work

    now starts

    a never ending reign."

He'll be born of me

    who knows no man.
The mother of the Son Most High

    whom God enthrones o'er all the earth.

How can this be?

    I'll never know.
Why should this be?

    I'll still never know!
Why such a poor and humble girl

    for such a high and mighty task!

But surely

    you must know.
You'd never ever make

    such a profound mistake.
How can it be?

    I'll never guess.

Many will not now believe
      that you should speak to me.
Not born in a palace
      or from a priestly line.
Not born to noble
      or to Pharisee.
I'm just an ordinary girl—
      from an ordinary family,
With an ordinary mother
      and an ordinary father.
With plain ordinary friends
      and with ordinary hopes.
          And ordinary . . .
              ordinary everything.

Isaiah prophesied so clearly,
      a virgin would the mother be
      of the coming great Messiah.
He foretold the day
      the babe would come;
He foretold the shadow,
      that the baby born
         would suffer
           and would die for all.

But that is something I can't see
          nor ever want to dream;
Though a spear
          my heart will pierce.

Now—I am yours
          in body and in soul.
I belong to you alone.
Just take me as I am.
Let what you will
          now happen.
My will
          is all your own.

I'll be your servant,
          Lord.
               I am your servant,
                    Lord.

Mary's Dilemma

I humbly submitted myself to the Lord,
  and lovingly accepted His sovereign will.
I'd endeavored to be good
  and honored my parents.
  I loved them
    and never would hurt them
    and prayed that I'd remain
      a good girl for them.
  I vowed I'd be obedient,
    a true child of the Lord.

But, then . . .
  I observed a change,
  a noticeable change,
    yet, ever so slight.
  The change was for sure,
    I knew I was pregnant.
      Oh! God be praised!
      It's just as You promised.

But . . .
  Who do I tell?
  When do I tell?
    I can't tell my dad,
      he'd never believe.
    I must tell my mother,
      she might believe.

But . . .

    When do I tell?

    How do I tell?

        I must tell the truth,

          I always have.

        Mum'll find it difficult,

            but I hope she'll believe.

Understand? No! . . .

    my mother couldn't.

Accept? I hope! . . .

    because she knows

    I've never been alone with Joseph,

        or any other man.

But the facts of life

    are against her believing

    that I'm still a virgin

    while a baby I'm carrying.

But . . .

    How do I tell?

    Why should I tell?

        I can hide it for now

          but soon it will show.

        Far better to warn her,

          than be questioned later.

But . . .

    Why should I tell her?

    What can I tell her?

       Mother, dear,

           I'm a loving daughter,

           faithful to you

           and obedient to God.

    Perhaps that's why He chose me

       to be a mother . . .

           to be the mother

           of his dear Son.

               His Son to be born,

               the Son—Emmanuel—God with us.

Mother?

    Please help father to believe

       there is no earthly father

       for the child I bear.

The Holy Spirit,

       the angel said,

       would overshadow me

       and cause me to be

       a virgin mother;

           for a virgin I am.

I humbly submitted myself to God,
and willingly accepted His will.
I'm the handmaid of the Lord
to do whatever He pleases,
to be the mother
of this world's Savior.

To Be The Dad

Oh, Dad,
    the news is bad . . .

It wasn't my creaking door,
    it was my bed on the floor
        rocking and scraping.
I was just tossing and turning,
    unable to sleep, Dad,
    because the news is bad.

It's Mary . . .
It's Mary . . .

I know the rumors are unreal
    and I'm afraid.
The rumors are saying
    that she's with child,
    and will deliver soon,
        don't swoon.
I wish I were dead
    before she puts to bed.

My boy, says Dad.
My boy,
    what have you done?

Dad . . . I . . .
Dad . . . I . . .
      it's nothing I've done.

You, says my dad,
      you're not innocent,
      she's obviously pregnant,
      and you are the . . .
         I can't say that
         about my son, sighs dad.

Joe . . . (that's my Mary)
I'm to have a child!

Yes, I know—
      I hope so, some day.

But Joe, (It's Mary repeating)
I'm to have a child.

When we marry someday, says I.
I too want a child;
      you will have many, says I.

Yes . . . but . . . (she stutters)
but I am . . .
I'm having a child . . . (she splutters)
I'm having one now.

You . . .
> with eyes fixed and brow pinched
>> I searched her eyes,
> somehow,
>> they proved her innocent,
>>> since that she was, and is.

My eyes met hers
> and love there was for me,
> and me for her.
My eyes descended from her facial beauty
> to her tummy.
Was it growing?
Then with eyes popping,
> and voice serious,
>> Mary, you can't,
>> you can't,
>>> this must be ended.

I'll tell you everything,
> she spoke so sweetly,
I'll tell you how this happened,
> she expressed it so tenderly.

No, don't!
> I can't believe that you could be
> unfaithful
>> like that to me.

Not unfaithful to you, my lord;
　　faithful, unto God, our Lord.

Don't blame God for that.
　　You, yourself, got that.

She told the whole—
　　she told me all the story.

I don't know.
I can't believe such story,
　　not now,
　　　　you know that.

Joe, you've disgraced our name,
　　it was dad again.
Go to, you must marry,
　　marry that girl quickly
　　and give the child a name
　　　　or send her away,
　　　　to a relative far away.

I'm not the father.
Believe me, Father.

Then break the vow,
　　don't marry her now.
It's not your child,
　　you're not the father.
　　　　Then who is the child
　　　　and who is the father?

God,
    she said.
God,
    that's who she said.
Oh, Dad,
    such excuse is bad.
        Who will believe her?
        I can't marry her.

At night
    I toss and turn,
    no wink of sleep,
    as in my mind
        I turn the thoughts of Mary,
        so soon to be a gentle mother;
    and with a child that's not my own.
        What should I do,
        instead of frown?

Go, my father said,
go to bed,
and in the morning we will talk again (if I'm not dead).
    How pleased I am to see him go,
        how pleased I'd be if I could only know
        what I must do.
            Yes, if I only knew
            what I must do.

What is that light . . . so unearthly bright ?

It gives me quite a fright . . . such a dazzling sight.

Be quiet!

Be still!

Don't fright, until you hear the news . . .

it is not bad,

but magnificently good.

People may think it bad,

the world will know it's good.

Now listen,

fear not,

Mary's child comes from God,

angels will proclaim good news to all,

about the Savior of the world.

God's gift of love,

a babe,

for you to love.

God is the father of this child.

Mary is not defiled.

You the earthly father are to be,

custodian of the child, from Me.

But,
      Father, I'm not the father.
He knows I'm not the father,
       He told me He's the father.
         God is the father,
           I'm not the father,
      but, I'm to be the father.
Believe me father.
I believe Him, father.
      The child to be,
      is God's child.

He called me mad,
      did my Dad.
He thought me bad,
      a big disgrace to be such a dad.
He was quite mad.

Me, bad?
A dad?

Mary,
      I'll be the Dad.

The Apprentice Angel

I don't know how they do it!
I don't know how they keep it up!
Singing! Praising!
Sometimes heralding!

Learning heavenly lessons,
    being taught how to apply them . . .
Hoping to be more harmonious
    on our celestial harps . . .
Practicing to perfect the immature noise
    too often escaping from cherubic trumpets . . .
Mostly learning the New Song
    that is forever new . . .
        even the old established angels
        are always learning this New Song.
Keeping up the reputation . . .
Measuring up to expectation . . .
    that earthlings have of our Angelic choir.

The joy of praise is early learned
    by an apprentice angel like me.
The ecstasy of praise,
    formally expressed,
    profoundly to enjoy,
        is but a small appreciation
        of our heavenly employ.

This "heralding" lark,
        some dare to say
        is for the birds—
            except, the birds can't sing,
            they only twitter.
                Whoever heard of a twittering angel?

"You are appointed for a special assignment."
        Such was the news
        being passed around the angels' quarters.
A Heralding assignment—
        that meant the usual group, plus one,
        always plus one.
            (The plus being the apprentice,
                and this time, it's me.)

It's exciting!
It's easy!
        Think of the privilege!
            What if I sing a wrong note?

Old Gabe, as he's affectionately known,
        will lead us off;
        then in one majestic cacophony of sound
            the message will be repeated
            and impressively emphasized by the rest of us.

At least,

    that's what the others say!

Gabriel has been entrusted with the message.

That means we are to herald some important happening.

    A prophet to be anointed?

    A monarch to be appointed?

    Some priest to be confirmed?

    Some leader to be affirmed?

This was to be one moment in eternity.

God's moment to change time;

    to send His Son

    as a love-gift to the world.

The trumpet sounds!

The heralds assemble—

    this time, I'm included.

The archangel is all resplendent in his sparkling attire.

God's blessing pours upon us all as we portray His Glory.

We are briefed regarding our earthly mission,

    sent to a cave-like dwelling

    in a town called Bethlehem.

    (I hope Gabe knows the way!)

Has he got lost?

    We are not in the town

    but over the fields.

They must be shepherds sheltering near those rocks.

They look chilly—tired of their silly flocks.

Gabriel starts.

    We all join in.

The shepherds quickly stir.

    Oh! How we scared them!

    They are really frightened . . .

        . . . and, I mean, awestruck!

            Perhaps they've never before seen an angel.

"Don't be afraid," said Gabe.

    That's all right for him,

    he's been brought up with cherubs and seraphs.

"I bring you good news."

    Does that mean the appearance of an angel

    is a bad omen?

"Good news of great joy for you and all people."

    I firmly said, Amen, to that.

"Today in Bethlehem,

    a Savior has been born for you,

    He is Christ, the Lord."

Then we all started singing—
"Glory to God on High."
　　I know that line—
　　it's repeated in every song we sing.
"Peace on earth,"
　　that's new!—
　　for a world torn apart with greed and strife.
"Goodwill to you men."
　　That made them sit up and listen.
　　　　So this is what heralding is all about!

"You'll find Him in a manger," added Gabriel.
　　That's no place for a baby, I thought,
　　even more so for God's precious Son.
　　　　But then, I'm not in charge.

After the message
　　we continued our singing.
The shepherds left,
　　we couldn't stop praising.
We all went to Bethlehem
　　and entered the town.
　　　　The angelic procession moved to a courtyard
　　　　and hovered above a stable manger.

24

Everyone saw the Christ Child,
    nestled warmly against His mother.
There lay the innocent infant
    possessed of Divinity.
The praises continued;
    the echoes crossed heaven.

I'm enjoying being an apprentice.
But never again
    will God's Son be heralded
    in the form of an earthly babe.
Yet on one great day
    we'll jubilantly burst forth again,
    when Jesus, the Christ,
    returns in His Glory to reign.

        (I'll have finished my apprenticeship then!)

The Shepherd Boy Left Behind

Lots of things are happening
    in Bethlehem this week.
Last night,
    angels were singing out in the fields.
Later last night,
    shepherds went baby-seeking in the town.

Today,
    things are not the same.
The old shepherds, who always grumbled,
    were positive and kind
    and praised us younger boys.
Yet,
    things are very much the same.
The sheep are just as silly,
    they bleat and wander,
        some end up stranded and lost.

A thing that never happens,
    happened late last night.
We shepherds had an angelic visit;
    they spoke to us direct.

It was frightening.
It was exciting.

I missed some of the excitement,
     because I'd run into the cave.
When I came out,
     the others were walking
        quickly towards the town.
I shouted to them
     to wait for me.
They turned and laughed,
     and said I was to guard the sheep.

Things haven't changed.
     I always get the dirty work,
     or miss the fun and pleasure.

They went,
     with the angels.
I stayed,
     with the sheep.
They saw a baby,
     where a baby shouldn't be.
I saw the stars,
     where they've always been.
In a stable manger
     was the new born babe.
The stars
     were in their usual place.

Today
    is different.
They are back at work;
    they've given me time off.
I'm going into Bethlehem;
    they can bleat with the silly sheep.

That baby must be different.
    Not just because
        He's surrounded by straw and cows.
    But because
        God sent an archangel to announce His birth.

I'm going now to see Him!
    I'll sing—or croak—
    some notes of adoration.
You see,
    I believe what the angel said—
        He is our nation's Messiah;
        He is our world's Savior.

I want Him to know
    I'm pleased He's come.

A Dog In Bethlehem*

There was a dog in Bethlehem!
    Well, there was . . . more than one.
There was a dog at Josiah's Inn!
    Well, there was . . . more than one.
There was a dog in his back stable!
    Well, yes, I was the one,
        and this is my story.

It was a strange night—
    the eerie sounds
    and funny sights
    from all around,
        just made me shudder.
            My hair stood on end;
            no wag in my tail,
                it only sagged between my legs.
            My ears were not sure what to do.
            With mouth wide open
                my tongue did what my tail used to do.
        I stood and shuddered.

The inn was filled with strange people
    with weird clothes
    and funny accents
    from many different places.

A strange young couple could find no lodging—
an awesome situation without any rooms,
she was in no state to be without a bed.
They came from Nazareth,
and were shown to the stable.

There was an abnormal commotion
stirred the air,
as angels sang,
while the babe arrived.
It was an extraordinary beginning,
just lying in a manger,
protected by a mother's love,
for the new born baby boy.

That new life,
we were told,
was God in human form.

That's mysterious . . .
That's profound . . .

But that's what I heard,
and am now telling you.

(*Author's Note: This could be used with a hand puppet)

31

More Than A Smile

If only I could speak

    and say more than a smile portrays . . .

I want to say, "Thank you"

    -to the mother who bore me.

I appreciate the angels

    that herald my birth.

The shepherds are kind,

    and the Magi generous.

But,

    then there is Dad,

    I'll call him that;

        though he's not my father

            he'll be a good parent.

If only I could speak

    and say more than a smile portrays.

The cattle are lowing,

    the sheep only bleat,

    the camels moan,

    the donkeys groan.

        I like those animals;

        they'll be my friends.

If only I could speak
     and say more than a smile portrays.

As a baby, I'll coo.
When a man, I'll grow.
     And as a man,
          I'll fulfill my Father's promise,
             to reveals His love
             and so share His grace.
I'll be His light
     in every dark place.

If only I could speak,
     I'd say much more than my smile portrays.

Give Him The Right Name

Alas!
    And what am I to say?
    Friends and family think me fiend
        and foe,
            to family, law and God.

Alas!
    They do not know—
    they refuse to hear what angel voices declared.
        Me they have not believed,
        but shun me to be cast out
            from family devout,
            and community so law abiding,
                for going ahead with wedding
                my pregnant betrothed.
        Proclaiming
        and maintaining
            her untouched virginity.

All lawful requirements have been fulfilled,
    Mary, now officially my wife,
        is mother of a child.
    A virgin she remained,
        as prophet had proclaimed,
        that a virgin would conceive
            and be the bearer of a child—a son,
                whose name and nature would suit God's plan
                of bringing redemption to a world He loved.

She is so beautifully innocent!
So magnificently pure!
So angelic to be a saint!
  God's rich blessing to outpour
  upon a sin-sick world,
    through the lowly maiden of the Lord,
    and by many to be adored.

Though Angels came and went,
  Mary is mine to stay—
  is mine for keeps.

The prophecies so remote,
  yet quite specific,
    mindboggling they may be
    but detailed to say the least
      as now they are applied
      to son and child in manger lying.

Though prophet had written,
  I needed the angel to speak
  quite personally to me.
What's written, he said,
  is being fulfilled.
He placed me by name in David's line.
  Joseph, he said,
    it's okay to take
    and now Mary your wife must make.

Promiscuous? No! Though pregnant, Yes!

    Pure she has been.

    Pure she was chosen.

        And pure she'll remain.

    The Holy Spirit is responsible;

        the offspring will be Emmanuel.

The angel had told me

    the son would be Savior,

    the expected Messiah,

        to be the Deliverer.

His name must be Jesus,

    His people He'll save,

    their sins will be dealt with

        by the son of my wife.

I'd never before seen an angel.

I'd never before heard from an angel.

    I'd heard much about them,

    but never encountered them.

We'd never known such angelic activity

    and all relating to God's nativity.

Almost inundated with angelic calls

    we appreciated each and every one.

        For Mary remembers—

        and so do I.

The angels told us separately,
    a son would be born;
        though not to have my family name.
    Proudly belonging to David's lineage,
        "Bar-Joseph"
            would naturally have been the choice.

Now that our baby is born
    a name must be given.
        "Bar-Jehovah,"
            supernaturally could have been voiced:
                Emmanuel,
                "God with us."

Jesus,
    must be the name
    by which He will be known.
There is no other choice.
    That name
        without a doubt
        is the name that must be used.

We have been told—
    so ours is the favor.
We'll give Him the name . . .
    "Jesus, The Savior."

The Magi

Wise Magi on their camels
    sought a new born king,
        made inquiries at the palace,
            told, no new born babe within.
Prophets were consulted—
    "Bethlehem's the place"—
        so they journeyed further,
        guided by the star.

Wise Magi from their camels
    descended to the stable,
    asked no further questions
        but gazed in awe and wonder.
Before a child of noble birth
    they bowed in adoration.

Wise Magi, while resting their camels,
    worshipped the new-found infant king;
    prostrate with pleasure,
    humbled their distinguished selves,
        allowed the crowns of pride
        to role from off their heads;
            and from their treasures
            valued gifts they gave.

Wise Magi, from their knees,
    remounted readied camels,
    returned home from pilgrimage so special
    rejoicing with many treasured memories.
        Predictions and prophecies had been fulfilled,
        Israel's king was born.

Wise human beings here today
    must seek Him on their knees,
    and, as they crown Him Lord,
        His blessings will receive.
Their faith journey now refreshed
with promises and covenant renewed,
    will throughout their life of praise ahead
        devoted pleasure give
        to their Master
        and their King.

Bow In True Humility

Kings may lose their crowns.
Magi lose their pride.
Shepherds pause 'mid midnight chores.
Angels praise from heaven's delight.

Soldiers, under orders,
    pursue to kill.
Visitors, under stress,
    stare in wonder.
Pilgrims, under compunction,
    race to view.
Followers, pause
    for covenant renewal.

Shepherds look with pleasure;
Magi lie prostrate and humble;
Kings must bow their knees;
While angels spread protecting wings.

All must bow,
    for this new babe
        is King of kings,
            the Christ,
            Emmanuel.

Christmas Thought

When you see a star,

                    think of the manger;

When you see a baby,

                    think of the Savior.

When you hear the angels,

                    then you start praising;

When you hear His Name,

                    then you too start believing.

When you see your presents,

                    think of your treasure;

When you see God's Gift,

                    think . . .

                    What can I give for His pleasure?

What A Christmas!

Christmas is over!
It may never have started!
 Preparations for feasting,
 preparations for merrymaking,
  all finished and complete.
   So, is Christmas over?

Business is booming
 for busy shopkeepers.
Their commercial enterprises
 give pleasing repercussions.
Extended trading hours
 result in better profits.
Prolonged advertising
 increases customer interest.
  Christmas for them
   makes the banks ecstatic.

The shoppers are tired,
 with cards, gifts, decorations,
 not to mention food and drink.
They'll be more tired
 with cash shortage
 and New Year bills.
  Christmas brought little blessing
  for them.

Tinsel has faded,
    candles burnt out,
    garbage bins over-loaded—
        What happened to Christmas?
Aspirins and Bismuth
    demanded by hangovers,
    fractured patience
        inflicted on spoilt, innocent children.
        What has Christmas done?

Presents have been opened,
    toys have been broken,
        it's certainly over,
        because it's washing-up time.

Carols have been sung or croaked,
    cards sent and received (maybe).
Then comes the echo—
    "Merry Christmas you suckers,
    you blearyeyed lot."
        Christmas never began!

It's almost over;
    all that remains is
    gluttony and intoxication.
        Christmas must be over . . .
        or it never began.

Christmas never began;
    never will begin
        until Christ is put back into Christmas,
        and takes His rightful place at your feast.
So,
    right now,
        where is Christ
           in your preparations?
    Where is Christ
           in your expectations?
    Will Christ be in your '99 Christmas?
Or,
    have you just not thought
    such a possibility could ever occur?

There is no Christmas
    for any one
    without Christ in His prominent place.
There is no Christmas
    for you
    until Christ is rightly in Christmas again.

Fasting

When you fast,

    don't look sour and gray.

When you fast,

    perfume your head and wash your face.

When you fast,

    don't beguile your friends

        with false gloom and sadness.

When you fast,

    reflect to them joyfully

        the Father's beauty and His peace.

When you fast,

    stay clear of the ashes and stinking sackcloth,

        which keep you dirty for many nights.

When you fast,

    sacrificially praise Jesus and enjoy His love,

        though it may last full forty days.

When you fast,

    let it not be for the praise of those who watch.

When you fast,

    let it be for God's joy and secret recompense.

Judas's Affection!

Let me demonstrate affection!
Let me come and kiss you, Master.
Come close,
       as when I followed close to you.
I heard you teach
       and walked with you.
I marveled at your wisdom
       and saw you heal.

       But, yet,
           I never loved you, Master.
           I never gave myself to you.
           I may have followed you
               along with all the others,
               but never gave my will to you.
           Your will was all Divine.
           My will was all, and only, mine.

You never moved Messiahship to acclaim.
The people you could so easily have won.
You could have claimed their crown
       and been upon the throne.
The kingdom could be yours alone,
       a kingdom all your own,
           with enemies dispersed
               and Romans fled,
           with infidels defeated
               and with praises fed.

But, no—
      you proved your weakness,
      your lack of zeal
         for freedom and for peace.
No longer zealous for our nation,
      your friends forsake
         and scatter far in fear.
You could have kept them—
      and me—
         and won the nation and the world.

Unacceptable were the people's hopes.
Untouchable were their methods sought
      for independence and for hope.
They longed for freedom, peace, and safety,
      but all you gave were pious platitudes
         of love, forgiveness,
            and no more hate.

Let me demonstrate affection!
Just a kiss,
      that's all I ask.
         The soldiers have their orders.
Jesus!
      let me kiss you now.
Betray?
      Yes!—that's the word.

Betray?
    It's all agreed,
        the price is paid.
        All that remains,
            is just the kiss,
                then you are theirs.

Affection demonstrated in this way
    reveals to them the Master,
        and hands you on to them
            to fight—
                or die.

His Darkest Night

Supper's not over,
I've been asked to leave,
   the others are staying, my absence they'll not grieve.
What I must do, the Master said,
   must be done quickly.

It really doesn't matter, what He said,
   it'll be done immediately.
The place was arranged—the time was set.
I met the priests—and the trap was set.
The price was agreed;
   their thirty pieces freed.
   The soldiers assembled,
   the march began,
   with torches and swords, through the streets, we almost ran.

I knew where to go—
   when they left the table,
   they'd proceed to the garden.
     Across the valley,
     amongst the trees,
     they'd be quiet—for a time of prayer.
They'd be tired—but He'd be there,
     to one side of the group as they froze;
He would be praying while the others doze.

I knew where to go,

    because there I'd betray Him.

    I'd been there before—

        I knew where to lead them.

Outwardly,

    to those who knew me,

    I was an intimate disciple.

Inwardly,

    to those who couldn't see me,

    I was an impatient disciple.

I, who had talked and walked with Jesus;

I, who had lived and worked with Jesus,

    was now

    a follower misguided,

        with a faith that had wavered.

I'm a Judean, my accent is different.

They're Galileans, their trades are different.

I'm interested in commerce, I have business agility;

with the others I'm contrasted, they've no accounting ability.

    I have ambition,

        yet with no fruition.

There is nothing
    in this wonder-worker:
There is nothing
    in this religious teacher.
With no prestige—no money,
with no future—no security,
    it's all just plain hard work.
My hopes of fame and fortune
    are unrealized, without extra work.

It's true,
    I'm a covetous man;
    a pilferer with a pious tongue;
    an embezzler with a pious song.
It's true,
    for avarice is my sin.
With a bribe,
    the price of a slave I'll hand Him over,
        Himself to save.
I'm not desiring his procrastination.
I'm not leading an insurrection.
He is no impostor for our nation—
    with this pressure, I'll get action.

"A traitor," did someone say?
"A loyalist," is what they ought to say.
    A loyalist is always more than loved.
    A traitor is nothing more than loathed.

With the symbol of love
    my Master I'd kiss.
With the expression of friendship
    His fate I'd fix.
        The kiss for the Master,
            was for identification.
        The arrest by the soldiers,
            was for interrogation.

I followed the torchlit procession,
    awaited the outcome of the unlawful occasion.
It was the farcical trial
    that made me rethink.
Seeing the innocent victim
    made my action stink.
So, filled with remorse and keen to atone,
        I said I was sorry;
        but it was only a moan.

I returned the money—the same thirty pieces.
"I have sinned, yes, I repent; innocent blood I've betrayed,"
    so went my report.

But they passed me by

> and refused to accept the returned silver pieces.

> > They had got what I had earned.

"What's that to us—we paid you the price,

> we've got our man—He'll be dead in a trice.

> > Your guilty conscience

> > matters nothing to us."

Jesus would forgive me,

> but I couldn't face Him.

He'd know my repentance was genuine,

> but I daren't go near Him.

> > Remorse holds me back.

> > I must stay away.

Oh, what have I done?

> I cannot escape my conscience so irritable.

> I cannot escape from the guilt so impossible.

> > Look at my pathetic state.

> > Penance can't change my fate.

> > > Where is the pardon my heart cries out for?

> > > Where is the power to change what was paid for?

What now?

It'd been better I hadn't been born!

What now?

Satan, you've achieved your goal!

What now? Or, what next?

There is this strong rope—

it'll hold me tight.

I'm now without hope—

it's a very dark night.

This Cup

Father, take this cup from me!

Though Your will must be done, not mine.

This cup is far too heavy for me.
    I'm about to be betrayed by one
        who has followed me throughout my ministry.
    He will not do it as an enemy would do,
        but with the gesture of a friend.
    I know I am to be denied by another close follower
        who says he would never do anything like that;
        yet he'll declare emphatically that he never knew me.
    I know also that within a short time all of my disciples,
        who are sleeping right now,
        will run away and desert me.

This cup is too heavy for me;
    Father, please take it away from me.

This cup is too heavy for me.
    I can see clearly that there is much suffering
        to be undertaken during the next few hours.
    I anticipate the horror of physical torture
        and a painful death.
There'll be much emotional anguish
and mental agony
    resulting from the trial and
    the ultimate rejection by Your chosen people.

This cup is too heavy for me,
 please let me escape.

This cup is too heavy for me.
 I know all that's going to happen.
 It'll mean the dreadful ignominy of a criminals death.
 I'll be taking upon myself the sins of the whole world.
 Ultimately that will lead
  to complete separation from You, my Father.
 Such is beyond comprehension.
  I do not want to anticipate it.
 I have always had a close
  and unbroken relationship with You.
That formidable moment is approaching when You will not be with me.
 The isolation of such a sacrifice will cut me off from You.

My Father,
 this cup is much too heavy for me to endure.

Father! . . .
 Father, is there no other way?

Father, not my will . . .

 Let Your will be done.

  Yes, Father, I accept the cup . . .

Left Alone

A man in the prime of life,
imprisoned for being innocent,
 forsaken by friends,
 beaten by soldiers,
 mocked by the scornful,
 ridiculed by God's chosen people.

By one betrayed,
by another denied,
 both were to blame
  in placing this victim into the hands
   of the irreverent religious regime.

Friends failed to visit Him,
enemies tortured Him,
priests tormented Him,
 while foreigners enforced the law.

Incarcerated and scourged;
 thirsty—while no one offered water,
 hungry—while no one broke bread,
 suffering—while no one comforted,
 lonely—while no one supported.

His friends,
 where have they gone?

His followers,
    where are they now?
        They broke bread
        and drank the cup
            at their last meal together.

But now—
    where are they?

          "A friend in need is a friend indeed
          when the need he seeks to meet."

The need was there,
    but where was a friend
    some deed to perform?

Friends were then unable to greet Him.
Followers then unable to meet Him.
    When in prison,
        they did not visit.
    When treated shamefully by foe and friend alike,
        no friendliness was offered.
    When held a captive,
        no followers joined to show support.
    When condemned,
        no comforter stood by.
    When soon to be executed,
        they'll all stand far away.

When He has departed,
    His followers will express their sorrow.
When away from earth,
    His friends will visit and encourage.

They will then have done it—just for Him . . .
    unwittingly they will have visited Him,
        because they would be ministering in His name.

Love For You

I love you—
Yes, I do!

    I taught you and I healed you;
        does this prove I love you?
    I lived with you and I cared for you;
        what more to prove I love you?

I suffered
    the scourge and the rod,
    the thorns and the nails;
        I'm dying a cruel death.

My anguish is yet deeper
    than the marks upon my flesh.
The hatred and the scorn—
    betrayal, rejection, and abandonment
    have scored their worst.
These scars within,
    in mind, in spirit, and in soul,
    will eternity outlast.

You see the wounds upon the skin,
    and yet the scars inflicted deep within
    are proof
        of Father's love
        and mine as well,
            and man's unloving inhumanity
            thrown at God's beloved Son.

But deeper still the hurt
　　of unrequited love,
　　　　spat right back.
Your spurning hurts
　　far more
　　　　than the flaying of the flesh.

I love you—yes, I do.

　　　　What more can be said?
　　　　What more must be done?

My passionate suffering,
　　precisely borne,-
　　　　is just for you;
This substitute death
　　guarantees life,—
　　　　personally for you.

Yes—
　　I love you.

With my last breath
　　I tell you again:
　　　　I love you,
　　　　　every one.

　　Still, yes,
　　　　I do.

His Death

Jesus died—
    sin condemned.
        Evil in every form
            is defeated through His death.
Deliverance through His death
    is now available for all who trust in Him.
        It was then—He died for us.
        It is now—we can live for Him.

Relief is found
    from overwhelming agony,
        in Christ the Savior's death.
Freedom is found
    and restoration given
    when,
        on the side of death—
            the other side of Christ's atoning Cross,
                we see the Throne,
                anticipate the glory
                    of life for ever more
                within the great Kingdom of our God.

For now,
    you may see some nails,
    and the wound the spear made,
    and around His head many thorns are crowned.

Yet,

    beyond the anguish and the pain,
    beyond the ignominious sight of death,
      and through the emptiness of tomb,
        so cold,
        so bare,
          comes life,
          abundant life—
            victory,
              and an eternal crown.

Silence At The Centre Cross

The air was silent.
The crowd was hushed,
Criminals' moans faded—.
Soldiers waited.

From the centre cross
  no sound was heard,
    the minutes fled
    and the hours passed.
The man was dying
  but he was not cursing.
There was the stillness
  of silence:
    the silence of eternity,
    the silence of time,
    the silence for sinners,
    the silence for saints.

All was silent at the centre cross.
The man was dying,
  but he was carrying
  the heaviest burden
  a God could bare.
He was accepting
  the ultimate fate
  by becoming sin.

He had crossed through the gate
from heaven to hell,
from being the Beloved
to now being rejected.

All was silent at the centre cross.
God's Son was dying.
In utter abandon
He had queried rejection.
"Why?
Why have you forsaken
your own beloved Son?"

The air was silent,
no voice from the clouds;
He was not at this moment
to be known by the crowds.

Five hours of silence
with added pain passed.
All that was left
was for breath to cease,
for lungs to collapse
with no strength to gasp.

With one final push
    on His nail-held feet,
        one painful inhaling
        and His lungs were filled.
With one last cry His mission fulfilled—
        "It is finished!"

And He gasped His last—
    His spirit left;
    and silence reigned.

The silence of time,
    the silence of eternity.
        The silence of sin's defeat,
           the silence of souls forgiven.
             Hell is vanquished!
             Heaven is opened!

All was silent at the centre cross.
But now great rejoicing
    by angels in heaven;
        sinners being reconciled,
        saints being glorified.
Thanks for that silence
    when Christ died our death.

The thunder cracked,
    the silence was broken;
        the Temple veil crashed
            the barriers trampled.

God broke through
    and silence was golden.

Mary At Calvary

"Dear Lady," he said,
and as he looked I grew more sad.
More sad, if that could ever be—
    I'd been sad for hours,
        since being told what had happened:
    "He's been arrested!", I was informed.

I couldn't imagine any charges being laid,
No laws could have been broken.
He came to fulfill, not break the law.

    He's been arrested!   By whom?
Not the Romans;
it must be the Priests.
    The Priests must be jealous,
        because he's a priest;
            at least so I believe.
My questions were answered,
And I feared the worst.

The cries of the crowd echoed and re-echoed.
    Hosanna! they had shouted;
        but that was last week.
    Crucify! was their latest cry;
        that was last night.
I couldn't believe it.
    The ones he had healed
    and the ones he had taught,
        how could they betray
        their friend and Messiah?

Crucify!
 And it wasn't the children playing at soldiers.
It was the leaders,
The national leaders,
Shouting for justice,
Demanding a killing,
Deliberately breaking the law they upheld.
 Exacting the death sentence.
 Demanding the shedding of innocent blood.
 Sarcastically insisting that his blood be upon them
 and upon their heirs.

The women came to me
 to comfort and weep.
We couldn't stay home.
 They tried to persuade me
 to stay home and mourn.
  But he's my son,
  I must be with him in his hour of need.
   This was his time of torture.
"Going there will torture you more,"
  was the comment of a loyal friend.
   I must be with him if he's going to die.
   He shouldn't die—he should live!
 They could not persuade me,
 Nor force me they wouldn't.
 So to Calvary we came,
  the dreaded Place of the Skull.

We could hear
    the blaspheming of the thieves.
We could hear
    the railing of the Pharisees.
We could hear
    the abuse from Priests and Scribes.
We could hear
    the crowd as they jeered and mocked.
        As closer we came
            we could hear the moans
            of those on the crosses
            to left and to right.

    And then the soldiers
        were hammering hard the nails
            that would hold my son on the cross.
I fell to the ground
    at the point of collapse,
as I felt those nails
    in my own hands and feet.
My friends knelt with me,
    then lifted me up when I said I must go.
        But not go home—
            go closer to my own loving son
            as they lifted his cross
            and dropped it
                hard into the centre hole.

Again I shuddered
    as the bones were jarred.
Again I trembled
    as his muscles pulled tight.
It was then I noticed
    the blood from the whippings
        so mercilessly given.
    The flesh had been torn
        with the thongs on the scourge.
It was then I saw
    the crown on his head,
        the thorns had torn his hair and his scalp.

My body was wracked with pain throughout
    and I remembered the word the angel had spoken,
        "A sword shall pierce deep down in your heart."

We stood
and gazed in utter horror—
    sheer disbelief that this was all real.
        But real it was, without a doubt.
And there were the soldiers
    with my son's tunic.
They'd shared out his garments,
    but this was the last.
        They wouldn't tear it,
           So they cast lots for it.

It was mine—
    I'd made it for him.
How I wish I could give him another
    to cover him now.
With shame I looked on the one I bore.
True to custom they'd stripped him bare.
    Now every one could see
    what they should not have seen.

There on the cross
    was my dying son.
Blood streaming down
    and flies on his wounds.
        Could I not just go and wipe those stains?
        Could not I just move those flies away?

My friends knew my thoughts,
    I could go no nearer.
        The soldiers wouldn't let me touch my very own son.

But I moved forward slowly
    and my friends moved too.
John was there to comfort;
    I could depend on him.

And then my son spoke.
    I strained to hear,
    so closer I went.

He looked straight at me
with love in his fading eyes.
"Dear lady," he said,
    so polite and considerate.
"Dear woman," was the phrase
    he used so endearingly.
He said it with feeling.
    It meant
    that I was his mother
    and held with respect;
        I was his mother
        so loved and so blessed.

"Dear lady, see your son,"
    his head turned slightly.
He looked at John.
Then told his follower,
    "See your mother."
As his eyes turned back
they expressed his love,
    which told me that John
    would take good care of me.
        In such moments of immense suffering
        his compassionate thoughts were for me.

John came closer
    as I slumped down again.
        I had cried and cried,
        now my tears seemed dry
        and refused to flow.

My heart was broken.
My strength had gone.

    John held me tight
    and turned me around;
        the others turned with me
        and we all walked away.

I paused,
and turned,
and looked once more.
    There on the cross
    in the heat of the day
    was my son—
        he was dying
        in an awful way.

My son?
    Yes!
    But God's Son as well.
        There on the cross
        was Emmanuel.

Calvary's Cry

Five hours of silence,
    six hours of pain.
Earth shattering silence,
    inexpressible pain.

Crucifixion's gory detail,
    rejection's mental anguish.
Emotions upheaval.
Love in reverse.
    Lungs collapsing—
    he's suffocating.

The cry of silence,
    the cry of pain.
Heaven's shattering silence,
    inexplicable pain.

Inner turmoil;
    spiritual distress;
    mental degradation;
    emotional lovelessness;
      rejected by God.

Right at the end,
    his emptying completed.
      Is he defeated?

The pain of silence,
   the silence of pain.
The burden of silence,
   unbearable pain
      of enduring hell,
      of becoming sin.
         Now, totally deprived
         of God's love and support.

The cry of pain,
   the isolation of pain.
Being a substitute—
   mankind's scapegoat.
Divine justice appeased
   by the sacrifice made.

Jesus became sin,
   and we cry with His pain.
He is our contemplation,
   our only expectation.

The cry of silence,
   the cry of pain.
      Earth's deadly silence!
      Eternal life's gain?

The silence shouts loudly.
After long hours of torture,
   the silence is broken
   with victorious acclaim.
      His mission is accomplished.
       Oh! Joyous refrain.

The silence of Calvary!
The sound of Glory!
   it is finished! -
      and sinners are saved.

We've Just Buried Him

The nails had been hammered,
    His flesh had been torn;
        the thorns had penetrated deep in His brow.
His blood had dripped
    from the cross to the ground.
The cross and the ground were cold and damp,
    stained with His blood
    and His life giving love.

The Lord who had healed
    the sick in their need.
The Savior who'd forgiven
    the guilty who feared.

    Now, nothing.—
Nothing but a body, lifeless and limp;
emaciated with scourge
    and torn by thorns,
marred with nails
    and violated with spear.

His body was pronounced dead
    by the officer in charge.
But He is God's Son!
    "He's dead . . .
        take him down,
        you have my permission."
Such was the authority given.

I looked for a partner . . .
    could anyone befriend
        the secret admirer,
        the night-time disciple?

There was a willing helper,
    Joseph by name, from Arimethea,
    who was truly a disciple,
    sincerely a friend.

Together
    we took Him
        down
        from the cross.

We levered the nails
    from His hands and His feet.
    We loosed the ropes
        and lowered Him gently,
        'til His body lay prostrate
        on the blood-seared earth,
            still wearing His crown.
He was truly a King!
    So, away went the thorns.

We had brought clean sheets
    for the customary use
    in enfolding a corpse.
Joseph had remembered
    the special sweet spices
    for wrapping between folds
of the burial clothes,
    as was the custom.

Now,
    where shall we lay Him?
        Joseph had it all planned!
        Nearby he had purchased
            a tomb for himself.
    "We'll use that for the King . . .
    the King of all Jews.
        It's not far away,
            we can carry Him there
            all by ourselves.
        The women who mourn
        will follow behind."

Never a body was carried
    with more dignity,
        more sorrow.
Never a man
    more honored,
        more loved;
Never more mourned,
    nor never more missed.

84

"The emptiness of life without the kind Master,"
　　so wailed the mourners.
"The emptiness of life without the Lord's love,"
　　bewailed his followers.

Then,
　　on to the tomb:
　　empty . . .
　　　　cold and bare.

We entered the tomb
　　with the corpse of the Lord
　　and laid Him down
　　　　on the inanimate bare slab.
　　We paid our respects,
　　then reverently retreated.
　　　　Sadly we rolled
　　　　the stone into place . . .
　　　　　　the tomb was sealed.

This looks like the end!
　　Jesus of Nazareth . . .
　　　　Is dead . . .

I know . . .
　　we've just buried Him!

Master!

Where is he?
Where have you put him?
Where is he?
What's happened to him?
　　Please take me to him!
　　I don't want to lose him!
　　　　I want to care for him!
　　　　I want to show my love for him!
　　　　　　I've done so before,
　　　　　　I must do so again.
I've asked you before,
Let me ask you again,
　　Where have you taken him?
　　Where is he now?

Through grief-filled sobbing
　　and with sorrow streaming down my cheeks;
　　　　for many hours
　　　　these tears have filled my eyes
　　　　and soaked my clothes.
　　　　My eyes are sore—
　　　　I can't see clearly in this morning light
　　　　just who you are.
　　But tell me please,
　　　　What must I do?
　　　　Who should I ask?
　　　　Where shall I go?

The grief-stricken streams
  flow down again.
The sad, bleary eyes
  fill up again.

If you're the gardener
    or a servant;
        you're the one I'll ask,
        you must know.
    Where is the one I've served,
        loved, honoured and adored?

He stood there—
    Oh, so patiently.
There never was a sneer.
    He so politely
        heard my lament
        and saw my misery.

He must have moved,
    Oh, so slightly.
He was about to speak
    and, Oh, so gently.

The tears my eyes had blinded.
The grief my mind had dulled.
    But when he spoke
    my soul awoke.

Just one word,
    that's all he uttered.
It was the word—
my heart was thrilled—
    it was my name.
"Mary," he said;
    and then I knew
        my grief would go
        and saddened tears no longer flow.

When with a shout
    my faith declared,
        "Rabboni!."

That's all it needed;
    my name from him,
my faith in him.

A gentle, personal touch—
    but he refused to let me touch.

    The word,—
    his voice,—
        just filled my need.
"Mary!—go and tell . . ."
    "Rabboni!—that I will."

Do Not Cling To Me

Death is no more!
Glory is on its way!

No going back to Crucifixion
    step ahead towards Ascension.

From gory detail of death's accursed hour,
    through cold dark deadliness,
        with rolling stone of Easter's light now gone
        is born a monumental hope
        of Eternity's long day
            of brightness, love and everlasting joy.

"Do not cling to me,"
    to re-establish memories of the past.
        For such joyful remembrances will not last,
        while shades of sadness momentarily will be cast.

"Do not cling to me."

    No longer rely upon the flesh,
        for touch and earthly contact.

        Be freed from death's chains.
        Be unfettered from death's sting.
        Find the wonder of unshackled freedom,
            the reality of life,
            abundant life,
                of life eternal.

Let the breath of Easter Joy and Resurrection Hope
        rest upon your frittered brow and sagging soul;
then forward go to your ascension
        into Beatific splendour;
        to my Heaven built room
                designed unequivocally for you.

"Do not cling to me."

        Proceed from Crucifixion's details most gory,
        to Ascension's prominent, prideful glory.
                Receive your liberty
                and with the wings of spirit given
                        fly onward, forward, upward
                                into the realm of life and light.

"Do not cling to me,"
        for we are free
        both you and me.

Alone

I sat in the corner
    all alone.
The others were together,
    but I was alone.
The others had lost
    the guilt previously born,
        Yet I was stranded
        and left alone with mine.
The others had received peace,
    while I needed proof.

They grumbled
    I'd absented myself from the supper.
They grumbled further
    because I had missed the Master.
He had blessed them
    and taken away their fright.
He would have blessed me,
    was their insistence.
        But I'm not trusting their account,
        I want proof for myself.

You may have heard Him;
    it could have been an echo of Him teaching.
You may have seen Him;
    It could have been a vivid memory re-seen.

I wont believe!
I want to see the scars from the nails.
I want to touch and assess their reality.
I want to see the wound in His side.
I want to touch and find the flesh real.
I don't believe!
I wont believe

Unless I see for myself.

I'm not trusting the eyes of others!
I wont believe the words of others!
I must see,

with these eyes of mine.
I must touch,

with these fingers of mine.

It was a lonely time.
The others were there.
I refused their comfort

and remained on my own.
There was no ostracizing

because I wouldn't conform

to what they claimed was fact

while I sought validity.

It was a long, lonely week.
>I dreaded more weeks to follow.

Lost in doubt and deliberate unbelief,
>the future looked hopeless.

The others were content,
>while I was unhappy.
>>They made me feel worse,
>>though insisted I stay.

It had been another dull day.
I anticipated a long, empty evening
>before retiring for an endless, restless night.

The others had made sure the doors were locked.
The Jewish leaders still offered a threat.
>We'd better be safe,
>with the bars in place,
>>than feeling sorry,
>>in their rough custody.

Suddenly,
>there was a weird, eerie atmosphere,
>sweeping through the room.

Some one had entered,
>but the door had not been opened.

Some one was inside
>who was not there before.

Then a voice,
    not a familiar disciple's,
    but a voice I recognized.
Then clearer words.
    my name was being used.
        The others sat silently,
        but listened and watched.
    I raised my head and moved my eyes.
        The others were looking in my direction.

Then more words were spoken,
    to me,
    and I looked up.
        He was standing beside me.
        I rubbed my eyes.
            He asked for my finger.
            He told me to look.
            He showed me His hands.
            He made bare His side.
                He told me to touch and to look.
        I saw for myself—
        I touched, to make sure.

"Stop disbelieving!" He gently rebuked.
"Start believing!" He loving encouraged.

      You must be my Lord!
      Yes!
          You are my God!

Peter

I'm only a fisherman.
    I know about bait.
I know how to catch
    the fish that will sell.
But, please stop that cock!
    It sounds like h---.
(That's what I would have said
    but now I wont.)

Stop that cock!
    It crows too loudly.
Stop that cock!
    I remember too clearly.
      He said I'd deny.
      I said I wouldn't.
        "You will," He said,
          "again . . . and again."
        "No, never, dear Lord,
          I'd much rather die."
    He knew me better
      than I knew myself.
        "You'll sit with the world,
        the enemies of God;
        you'll curse you don't know me
        and never been with me."

"I command you to witness,"
　　the Lord had said.
"You'll deny even knowing me,
　　and you'll be sad."

Oh! Stop that cock!
It's early morn.
Please stop that cock,
　　it makes me mourn.

He said I'd be sad,
　　but I'm even more mad
　　that I hadn't the courage
　　to stand for my Lord.

Commissioned to witness
　　at home and abroad;
　　and I couldn't say,
　　　"Yes. I know the Lord."
Three times I said,
　　"No! I know not the man
　　of whom you speak
　　and torment me so."
　　　"Dear girl . . . shut up . . .
　　　just leave me alone
　　　to sit and be warm
　　　　by this glowing fire."

Three times I'd said, No!
Then the cock started to crow.
    Oh! No! . . .
        He said I would.
            I denied knowing the Son of God.

I started to cry . . .
    that's not like me,
        a fisherman brave during storms at sea.
I cried with tears,
    my face was wet;
        and then I felt
            not a touch,
            but a look.

I wiped my eyes
    and glanced around;
        there stood the Master
            looking my way.
It wasn't for long . . .
    a brief passing moment.
It was a look that said,
    "I knew you would."
It was a look—
    it melted my heart.
It was a look—
    He was very sad.
I was sad,
    and I cried again.

It was a look of love . . .

    so sincere.

I immediately turned

    and ran out of sight

    and into the night.

I, who once said,

    I would not deny,

        now fled away

    and wanted to die.

I had boasted allegiance

    to Jesus the Christ;

        I would never deny,

        I would much rather die.

Stop the cock . . .!

    I remember too often.

Stop the cock . . .!

    I cannot forget.

        I remember His eyes,

        I relive that look,

            He knew,

            He always knew;

                He knew what I'd do.

But He said I would turn
    and then be strong;
        turn from myself
            and strengthen my friends,
                turn full circle
                and serve the church.

Yet, back to the boat
    and the fishing again;
    other disciples came back
        and we fished again.
We caught no fish,
    they just weren't there.
We pondered afresh
    what the Lord had said,
        "You'll be empowered,
        you will catch men;
            not for your pleasure
            but for my Kingdom."

Then, there on the shore
    a stranger shouted,
        "Throw your nets from the other side."
What does he know?
Yet, we tried . . .
    We had struggled all night
    without a bite;
        now the nets strained,
        they were full and began to break.

"It's the Lord!

It must be the Lord."

So, in to the shore the boat we rowed,

dragging the nets with the fish enclosed.

Breakfast was ready,

we all sat and ate.

No one queried;

we knew who He was.

He took me aside—

embarrassed I was.

As we strolled down the beach -

ashamed I became.

He gently asked If I really loved Him.

"You are my friend."

"But do you love me?"

"You know I'm your friend."

"But do you love me . . .

. . . just as a friend?"

"You know what I mean . . .

you know all about me . . .

I do love you, Lord."

Three times He had asked.
    Three times I'd denied.
    Three times I refused
        to speak up for Him.
Three times He now asked
    if I really loved Him.
He knew all along the response I would make;
    He commissioned me again, disciples to make.

"Feed my sheep,
    and feed my lambs—
        a very good shepherd you will make
            when the Spirit descends
            and makes you a saint."

Still there is pain
    when the cock crows again.
I am reminded each morn
    how I denied knowing Him;
        how ready I was to walk away,
        while He went to die.

But,
    now there is a boldness
        I had never imagined.

Now,
    when the cock crows
        I thank the dear Lord
            that He loved
            and forgave.

I was Peter . . .
    the fisherman;
        overly impatient and earnestly brave.
I am Peter . . .
    the shepherd;
        willing to die and ready to save.

The Ascension of Jesus

Atop the mount
    a cloud descended.
The Master hidden from their eyes,
    began to rise
        and trepidation filled their hearts
        as the Disciples said farewell.

From beside the cloud
    the Angels spoke.
        "Stop star gazing!"
But even such a word
        did not impede their gazing higher.

From beside them on the mount,
    the Angels asked why
they continued to look up into the sky.
    "Men of Galilee,"
    that's who they were.
    "Why stand gazing thus?
    This same Jesus who is going,
    will appear again one day."

From beside them came such words
    they found difficult to understand,
until they knew He'd promised
        to return from Glory just for them.
That's why the Angels said,
        "In just the same way as you have seen Him go;
        He will come back again."

Their hearts were down
　　　as He was lifted up.
When descending from the mount
　　　new hope arose.
　　　　　Then began the patient waiting
　　　　　for the promise to receive;
　　　　　　　and after anticipative vigils
　　　　　　　　the Holy Spirit came
　　　　　　　　and power was theirs.

Our Lord is standing
　　　at his Father's Throne;
　　　the stance of blessing
　　　　　gives us hope of reaching heaven too.

He prays His priestly prayer
　　　that we might holy be;
　　　　　united with His brethren
　　　　　　　is His desire for you and me.

And we too must watch and wait,
　　　for the appearing of our Lord;
　　　for He is coming back for us,
　　　　　to take us to the place prepared.

Waiting

Wait! Wait! Wait!
Why did He tell us all to wait?

Disciples wait upon their Lord;
     He's their example and their pattern.
Their decision;
     decidedly to be like Him.
His desire,
     that they be less like self,
     and more like Him.
People then will clearly see
     how diligently they have tried;
     how faithfully they've followed Him.

Servants wait upon their master,
     always at his call and beck.
They themselves are never free;
     never free to please themselves,
     never free to speculate;
       always bound—
       never again to be themselves,
         with no free time to brood.

Tax collectors never wait.
     Payment;
     whenever paid
       'tis always late.

The people are afraid,

    how could a Roman servant

        find contentment?

    How could a well-known cheat

        ever change and have to wait?

Fishermen! that's a different story.

    Patience? Yes!

        Especially when the fish wont bite.

Waiting? Yes!

        That's their role in life to play.

        That's what fishing's all about.

Waiting, hoping there'll be a catch today.

        Fishermen have a waiting story.

Wait! Wait! Wait!

Why did He tell us all to wait?

In your weakness,

    ineffective you will be.

In your sadness,

    hindered from being truly free.

        So you are told

        to wait, and be made bold.

Tarry in the city,
    wait a few more days.
Now you're wallowing in self-made pity
    then you'll jump and shout and praise.

Wait! Wait! Wait!
Why must we in the city wait?
    In these crowded streets
      we feel more fear.
    In the great metropolis
      we cannot yet feel free.

Wait in the city!
    It's easier said than done.
Wait in the city!
    How many days are still to run?
He tells us all to wait
    until from heaven the power's received.

What does He mean?
    The power?
      The power He promised
        with His Spirit.

So,
    all we must do
      is wait . . .
        . . . and then receive.

You Shall Receive

"You shall receive,"
   that's what our Savior promised.
"Power from on high,"
   that's what our Lord promised.

      He had died.
      They had buried Him.
      He rose again.
      We had seen Him.

What tremendous joy
   dispersed our sadness.
What momentous ecstasy
   accompanied the banishment of all our fears.
      He was alive!
         But then . . .

Then He left us once again;
   ascending with angelic escort
   into the realms of Heaven's glory.
We gazed . . . and gazed . . .
   The Angels told us not to gaze.
We gazed . . . He disappeared,
   and we were told He'd come again.
      That is now our hope,
      such is our expectation.

He had said,

    "You shall receive power from on high."

But, when Lord?

    We are weak and powerless.

    When will the power be given?

        "You shall receive . . .

        when the Holy Spirit comes upon you."

We had heard about God's Holy Spirit.

The Master taught us much.

    But still we wondered:

        How shall we know?

        What will happen next?

        Will we be very different then?

We had waited many hours

    and nothing had happened.

We had waited forty days

    and we were still the same.

        But He had promised,

        so we believed and waited with growing expectation.

He had promised—

    we would receive.

It was a quiet start
    with the new sun shining,
    warming the chilled night air
    and bringing sleeping things to life.
This was a day like all the rest.
We had gathered, and we had prayed.
    We had done it all before.
    Our prayers were just the same.
        Except on this morning
        we prayed with more fervor.
    We didn't know why, it wasn't contrived.

The peace of the new morning
    had imparted new peace within.
The tranquillity of dependence . . .
    the gentle vibrating air of expectancy . . .
        now breezed through each one of us
        as together we prayed and continued to wait.

There was a quiet interlude,
the stillness overcame us all.
    Then a movement—but not from us.
    Then a sound—not one of us spoke.
    Then a sparkling light—no one moved.

The sound, the sight, became more intense.
The sight and sound
   developed more dramatically
   until each one of us realized
   a sense of newness surrounding us.
        The sound had started like a breeze,
        it now increased into a mighty wind.

The searing sight of flames encircled all
   with the orange and the reds
   and the yellows in between.
The tongues of fire did not consume,
   but sat upon each one.

We looked . . . and looked again!
   What was this marvelous sight?
   What was this rushing sound?

The promise had at last been given.
He had foretold we'd be empowered.
   Was this the Spirit
        our Lord declared would fall?

We felt a difference—we saw a difference.
   A new language and determination.
   A new enthusiasm and disposition.
   A new surge of power and enabling gifts.
   A fuller understanding of worship
        and nobler expressions of praise.

We had been filled with His Holy Spirit
　　and were now more eager
　　　　to preach and to teach,
　　　　to heal and to save.

We had been made anew!
We had been given life!
　　Jesus had promised we would receive,
　　　　And this is it!